D1549174

Poets
to the People

Poets
to the People
South African Freedom Poems

Edited by Barry Feinberg

Foreword by Hugh MacDiarmid

London George Allen & Unwin Ltd
Ruskin House Museum Street

First published in 1974

This book is copyright under the Berne Convention. All rights
are reserved. Apart from any fair dealing for the purpose of
private study, research, criticism or review, as permitted under
the Copyright Act, 1956, no part of this publication may be
reproduced, stored in a retrieval system, or transmitted, in any
form or by any means, electronic, electrical, chemical,
mechanical, optical, photocopying, recording or otherwise,
without the prior permission of the copyright owner.
Enquiries should be addressed to the publishers.

ISBN 0 04 808020 9 hardback
     0 04 808021 7 paperback

821·08
FEI

Printed Offset Litho in Great Britain
in 10 point Times Roman
by Cox & Wyman Ltd, London, Fakenham and Reading

To South Africa's political prisoners and to the African National Congress and its allies

Proceeds from the sale of this book will go to the International Defence and Aid Fund for its continued work in Southern Africa

Acknowledgements

Thanks are due to Heinemann for extracts from
A Simple Lust by Dennis Brutus and *Dead Roots* by
Arthur Nortje; to Andre Deutsch for extracts from
Zulu Poems by Mazisi Kunene; to Oxford University
Press for extracts from *Sounds of a Cowhide Drum* by
Oswald Mtshali; to Renoster Books, Johannesburg
for extracts from *Yakhal 'inkomo* by Wally Serote;
to Lawrence & Wishart for extracts from *Apartheid*
edited by Alex LaGuma; to the editors of *The African
Communist*, *Sechaba* and *Anti-Apartheid News* for
various poems extracted from their respective journals.

Contents

Foreword
by Hugh MacDiarmid

If I had known nothing about the development of the protest literature sampled in this collection, and nothing about the South African liberation movement it represents, I could have hardly begun to read through it without recognizing that it powerfully emphasized the sense of that superb specimen of contemporary graffiti which runs: '"Mr Gandhi, what do you think of western civilisation?" – "I think it would be a good idea"', and alongside it, to account for the acquiescence of so-called, or self-esteemed, civilized people in the appalling iniquities of the system, might well be put this other one, which reads: 'God *is* alive – He just doesn't want to get involved'.

There can be no greater mistake than to criticize these poems for not answering to the requirements of what reactionary academics regard as 'high poetry'. I am sure my friend, that great linguist, the late Professor W. J. Entwistle, who, when he wrote his great book, *European Balladry*, describing the interaction over the centuries of the ballad literatures of the European countries, replied to the criticism of the bulk of ballad verse that it was deficient in aesthetic value by saying:

'If we are to measure by an absolute poetic standard, no doubt – and if, perchance, such a standard exists. The classic and the critic demand the application of such standards; but the search for a poetry that shall be pure dissolves even the greatest works of art into unrecognizable fragments. . . . The poetry of the commonalty we neither produce nor admire. Those who seek to express what many men feel we the more likely esteem for their art; while, on the other hand, the tribe of those who refine and polish and sublimate their art is left to prophecy to the void. It is not so that much of the world's greatest poetry has been composed, and it is not the way of the ballad. The greatest poets have written neither to extrovert their personalities nor to comply with the demands of taste, but to voice the common thought of masses of men. . . . There have been great poems which can be assessed as "pure poetry", such as the *Orlando Furioso*; but to the men of the sixteenth century Ariosto's masterpiece seemed wanting in substance or seriousness. We cannot be sure that it expressed something clamouring for utterance:

Glory and generous shame,
The unconquerable mind, and Freedom's holy flame

But these are the themes of a "God-gifted organ-voice", and these, rather than absolute perfection, assure survival in literature. And common, fundamental, moving themes of this kind inspire the best of the ballads. . . . It has been worth while to recreate them time and again throughout the centuries, since on each single occasion they have signified something to their unlettered bearers, and have moved them more than a trumpet. It is a glory not often achieved by the great artistic poets, and, when achieved, it is through some partial endowment of the generous ballad simplicity.'

Bourgeois writers and readers may decry 'commitment' in poetry, but they have not been subjected to the intolerable pressures which render it unavoidable and invaluable. It is still too widely believed that great literature is a prerogative of the Big Five, but 'the race is not to the swift nor the battle to the strong', and all over the world today millions of people, feeling they have been cut away from their real roots, are striving to re-root themselves in their native languages (even when these have been long obsolete or obsolescent, and never previously media of any written literature; and are seeking to create new indigenous literatures on the basis of their native traditions). The contemporary Scottish Gaelic poet, George Campbell Hay, in a brilliant essay on 'Gaelic and Literary Form' put the whole matter into a nutshell when he said:

'The slash at the "general stream of European literature" as understood by people like Quiller – Couch (whom I choose as a particularly horrible example) and as embodied in tomes with that title, a selected list of countries and a selected list of names from each of these countries, starting of course with the Greeks, well-bowdlerized into "Christian gentlemen" is a ramp that no longer impresses – like "Western Europe". I am all for the "minor literatures" and the "backward races", whose literatures have not been "etherealized" out of life. Our contacts might as well be with the Islaendings or with those great rascals the Serbs as with Bloomsbury or the Seine. The big countries share a common foreign-ness and repulsiveness to me, and like Wilfrid Scawen Blunt I sometimes wish they would destroy one another.'

This collection heartwarmingly demonstrates the great ground for hope expressed recently by a reviewer of 'the flowering of Russian poetry' when he wrote: 'What always seems so contra-

14

dictory and yet so reassuring is that in no matter what country, Communist or Capitalist' [And this book shows throughout Africa too] 'a poet is the same, the same breed continues to love beauty and hate oppression, to believe in spiritual values and the mind's affinities, to recognize and appreciate each other in "this terrible age" (Akhmatova), "the age rocking with the waves of man's anguish", when "above the black river the transparent spring has been shattered and the wax of immortality is melting."'

I express my solidarity with, and send my fraternal greetings to, all the contributors to this volume. We shall overcome!

Hugh MacDiarmid
Biggar
Scotland
March 1974

Introduction

Modern South African poetry has always been circumscribed by the ideology and operation of racial elitism. Apartheid laws, through many layers of social and cultural application, have effectively insulated the creative arts against black penetration and influence. With very few exceptions recognition of black poetry has been confined to those forms which tend to reinforce tribalism and white paternalism.

White poets have helped to strengthen their privileged exclusiveness by pandering to the exigencies of Apartheid. Apart from time-serving hacks, there are many poets who give unconscious support to the present structure of South African society through their quiescent life style and political apathy; a situation which cannot but infect the content of their writings. Others, less conservative, opt out of conformity into an amorphous 'avant garde', borrowing European and American styles of abstraction and aestheticism, which the Apartheid state is flexible enough to accommodate.

In recent years, in harmony with the upsurge of revolutionary spirit among the black majority, there has been a vigorous and unprecedented growth of radical, socially committed poetry. Long denied an outlet for cultural expression, the voice of South Africa's impoverished millions is now being taken up and articulated by scores of angry young black poets. Some 200 of these new poets submitted their work for the 1973 Roy Campbell Poetry Award along with 400 white contestants. The Award committee refused to consider the work of any black poet and bluntly rejected, out of hand, all 200 entrants.

While a handful of black poets have been published by certain courageous liberal presses still tolerated by the Government, it is clear that nothing short of the demolition of white supremacy will help to achieve an authentic South African culture in which poets of all colours will flourish. Those poets, black and a few white, who have attacked the existing system have recognized the essential unity of cultural and political freedoms. They have, as a result, been hounded and mostly dispersed abroad, though not for their poetry – which would seldom have seen the light of day – but for their political actions against the racist State.

The poets of this volume have all endured persecution and

official censure of one kind or another including, for some, imprisonment and torture because of their beliefs. It is because of their beliefs that they write as they do and it is because their writings consistently and eloquently echo both the problems and the deepest yearnings of the victims of Apartheid tyranny that they are included in this compilation.

This is the first anthology of poems projecting the alternative, revolutionary voice of South Africa. These ten poets have all been fired by their national realities, realities which are not only daily dominated by the brutalities of Apartheid, but are also witness to the gathering forces which must inevitably destroy that system. Of the ten poets only two, Mtshali and Serote, live in South Africa. Theirs are among the most powerful and lyrical voices being raised above the squalor of South Africa's black labour reservoirs. The eight exiled poets have been based mainly in London; one of their number, Arthur Nortje died tragically in 1970 while studying at Oxford University.

The lines of the South African conflict are already sharply drawn. With the intensification of the fight for a humane and egalitarian society comes an increasing need for South African poets to identify themselves with the aspirations of the majority of their people, and therefore with the aims of the national liberation movement, the African National Congress. Only through directing their talents against Apartheid, by placing the misery of the oppressed into a perspective full of hope and action, can South African poets help to forge a democratic society and culture in their country.

The poems in this volume are a beginning; they offer a foretaste of the future; they amplify the embryonic voice of tomorrow's South Africa.

Barry Feinberg

Dennis Brutus

FOR A DEAD AFRICAN[1]

We have no heroes and no wars
only victims of a sickly state
succumbing to the variegated sores
that flower under lashing rains of hate.

We have no battles and no fights
for history to record with trite remark
only captives killed on eyeless nights
and accidental dyings in the dark.

Yet when the roll of those who died
to free our land is called, without surprise
these nameless unarmed ones will stand beside
the warriors who secured the final prize.

[1] *John Nangoza Jebe: shot by the police in a*
Good Friday procession in Port Elizabeth 1956

I AM THE EXILE

I *am* the exile
am the wanderer
the troubadour
(whatever they say)

gentle I am, and calm
and with abstracted pace
absorbed in planning,
courteous to servility

but wailings fill the chambers of my heart
and in my head
behind my quiet eyes
I hear the cries and sirens.

THE SOUNDS BEGIN AGAIN

The sounds begin again;
the siren in the night
the thunder at the door
the shriek of nerves in pain.

Then the keening crescendo
of faces split by pain
the wordless, endless wail
only the unfree know.

Importunate as rain
the wraiths exhale their woe
over the sirens, knuckles, boots;
my sounds begin again.

AT A FUNERAL[1]

Black, green and gold[2] at sunset: pageantry
And stubbled graves: expectant, of eternity,
In bride's-white, nun's-white veils the nurses gush
    their bounty
Of red-wine cloaks, frothing the bugled dirging
    slopes
Salute! Then ponder all this hollow panoply
For one whose gifts the mud devours, with our hopes.

Oh all you frustrate ones, powers tombed in dirt,
Aborted, not by Death but carrion books of birth
Arise! The brassy shout of Freedom stirs our earth;
Not Death but death's-head tyranny scythes our
    ground
And plots our narrow cells of pain defeat and dearth:
Better that we should die, than that we should lie down.

[1] Velencia Majombozi, who died shortly
after qualifying as a doctor
[2] Colours of the African National Congress

20

TODAY IN PRISON[1]

Today in prison
by tacit agreement
they will sing just one song:
Nkosi Sikelela;[2]
slowly and solemnly
with suppressed passion
and pent up feeling:
the voices strong and steady
but with tears close and sharp
behind the eyes
and the mind ranging
wildly as a strayed bird
seeking some names to settle on
and deeds being done
and those who will do the much
that still needs to be done.

[1] *26 June 1967, South African Freedom Day*
[2] *Nkosi Sikelela Afrika = God Save Africa (the anthem of the
African National Congress)*

FOR CHIEF
(*A Tribute to Albert John Luthuli died July 1967*)

1

So the old leonine heart is stilled

the grave composure of the carven face
matched at last by a stillness overall

the measure of bitterness, totally filled
brims to the tautness of exhausted space

and he who sustained a faith in grace
believing men crippled could still walk tall
in the thorn-thickets of corrupting power

and more dear the central humanity
than any abstractions of time or place
daring to challenge, refusing to cower

mangled even at the end, he lies quiet
his stillness no less an assertion of faith
and the indestructible stubbornness of will.

2

So the machine breaks you
and you fall
still fighting grimly

the years epitomize
in this harsh act
of many:

Should one despair
knowing how great the power
how unavailing opposition?

Yet your great soul
asserts a worth –
transcendant humanity.

There is a valour
greater than victory:
   Greatness endures.

3

And the people mourn
the millions mourn,
the sorrowing land
is plunged in deeper sorrow:

When will the soft rains dissolve the entire landscape
    at dusk?

Sorrow and anger stir,
Dull pain and truculent woe,
and bitterness slowly seethes
till fury cauldrons from pain –

Oh when will the blind storms rampage the landscape in
    the dark?

4

Return to us

when sunset smoulders on the smooth horizon,
when the trees are starkly black
and beautiful
against the red and mauve of the sky

Return to us

when woodsmoke comes sweet and poignant
from the fields at dusk
after the winds of our fury have breathed
on the smouldering coals of our anger
and our fierce destruction has raged

O great patient enduring spirit
return to us.

5

O grave and statuesque man
stand along our paths,
overlook our ways

goad us by your calm regard
fire us with your desire,
steel us with your will.

Spirit of freedom and courage
guard us from despair
brood over us with your faith.

Fire the flagging and the faint,
spur us to fierce resolve,
drive us to fight and win.

6

And you
my friends
my allies
cosily chaired in London
or termiting in a thousand towns
or treadmilling the arid round
of protest, picket, pamphlet –
for as long as fervour lasts:
what shall I say of us?

O let Chief's reflected splendour
and the aura resistance sometimes brings –
except to the jaded, jaundiced, cynic –
o let us catch a little of this fire
and let us burn and steadily assert
our faith, our will to freedom and our love
for freedom and our dear unhappy land:
of inextinguishable and hungry fire
of love and hunger and imperishable resolve.

7

And the men
the dear lonely men
gaunt, and with a hunger around the eyes,
and the busy women
friendly strangers in a hundred lands:
ah these, my comrades and my friends!
how long, oh how much longer must it be?
how long still the wrench at throat
the pluck at eyes
at mention of some small forgotten word –
Fietas or Woodstock or Gelvandale – ?
how much longer must we doggedly importune
in the anterooms of governors of the world
or huddle stubborn on the draughty frontiers of
        strange lands?
how long must we endure?
and how shall I express my gratitude and love?

THE GUERILLAS

(For the fighting men in Southern Africa)

1

. . . and I lie with my body curved to the light clay
and it lies along the length of my hip and thigh
like the yielding firmness of your warm flesh:
and my body melts with a tenderness along my frame
while brittle thorn-twigs pierce the clear sky
while far-off sounds – harsh birds – blunderings –
      crackle like snapped twigs . . .
and ants scurry on the smooth curve of the clay

2

. . . the birds wheel in their great circles in the mind
heat beats at the eyes through a curtain of sweat
the salt-tasting mouth is papered by thirst and other things.
In time, heat and fatigue
will beat the stiff, anxious, aching neck down

3

. . . a sense of lost opportunity like a squall of rain
marching away leaving an aching hollowness
while the big ants crawl over the torn flesh
and the black streaks of crusted blood.
Who will break through the barriers
of indifferent bone and stubborn flesh
and the grey waves of newsprint gruel?
O my friends where are the voices to plead your cause
to roar your challenge
to trumpet your heroism?
to speak the words of brave resolve
that you live and die.

4

There is such a pleasure at last
in handling a cool efficient weapon
most modern, highly automatic
and moving off at the ready –
wishing they could see at home – the friends
and especially the children,
and imaging the deeds of flame and terror
– terror from this weapon, terrible and cold.

5

Chiefly it is a job to be done,
with drills to be followed and observed,
the enemy an analysable factor
or a brute so deadly that he *must* die first:
but sometimes there comes the thought of home
the angry longing of the exile
and a fierce will to smash an evil cruel thing.

Barry Feinberg

SURPRISINGLY SINGING

While whites
on sabbath greens
slowly bowling,
on weekdays
growing gold,
back home
black men
break backs,
surprisingly
singing.

STATUE TREATMENT

Statue treatment
(politely called):
a chalk circle
not caucasian
of Brecht derivation
but a crude elipse scrawled
on corridored floors.
Queues form to fill it
none moves slower
more slightly
one by one
week by week

Those who wait
may sit
sleep or urinate
but once in
once embraced by
that small smudged boundary
no clock to match
the move of life
only pulse at throat

throbbing thighs
toes splintered
by shifting weight

Above all the light
full sun power
unblinkered
paling ebonies
to ivory glint.
Phantoms surround
teeth rasping
jaws raging.
Sagged muscles
switch roles
voluntary to
involuntary
arse from elbow ill-defined
knees to gravity bend
bladder by dignity holding
lashed water to face
brings back focus.
No bruising bone
no crude bash
crushing kidney
no disfiguring attack
by strict instructions
only senses assaulted

Sight and sound suffer
smell is plain of sweat
feel is head enlarged
hands diminished
feet disappearing

This for a name
a time
a place who with
a secret rhyme
a riddle learnt.
When even on those
long-lit nights
this vomits out
the hate is held
an idea with fury kept.

TEN TARGETS REEL UNDER RAGE OF VISION

After years of bruising loads
heaved picks and burning girders,
knotted limbs and bitter knuckles cracking,
a gun lies lightly on the shoulder.
A big gun of many assemblies,
smooth bullets coil toothing at the neck,
grenades hung from hip gently swinging.

Once a volunteer under Gandhi colours,
head bleeding from double bludgeon
for turning cheek to set right thinking.
Then haunted by post-midnight squads,
splintered doors, splattered walls,
kicks and children clinging.
Years of guards beating in bleak yards,
conscience brothers thinned and shaking,
some, green veined on electric charges,
another, crazy dangled by borrowed belt.

This felt a thousand times repeated:
sons long left to memories yearning
a face loved, fades while reappearing,
home, a mirage of vapoured living.

Now,
memories feed round embered flame,
an Impala, fresh impaled, fat sizzles
burning carbon crust to stay a day's march.

Tomorrow,
maybe no game but combat coming.

Then,
that fast drop to knee
fierce burst of fire,
quick dodge and crawl
and back track to cover.

This,
a fine tuned, harsh handled man
hard as nails and head well guided;

no computer type reaction
no lathe like operation,
but thought out, mind planned,
hands trim on hair-taut trigger.
His eyes blaze down dead-still barrel,
ten targets reel under rage of vision.

J. B. MARKS:[1] an epitaph

He was a mountain of a man,
a Kilimanjaro rampant
in our ceilings furthest reaches.
Forged from burning rock,
that no winter blast
could freeze the ploughed-up brow,
or smooth the craggy buttress of his bones.

Fissures mapped his burnished jaws
like eroded beds, once coursing tears
bled in youth, then crusted
by the lava flow of life.

All men called him uncle,
not in sermon or religious embrocado,
rather awe and easy affection:
an echo to the timbre of his heart,
an accent to the legend of his name.

A kindly philosopher,
a knight of Lenin's table,
a man who wanted all men well.
But now that his rumbling recedes
and his fight of fights is over,
let's look (as he once did)
to others among us!

[1] 1903–1972. Chairman of the South
African Communist Party and a leading
member of the African National Congress

A COUNTERPOINT OF MARCHING FEET

(*to the black workers of Durban*)

We will
remember Durban
in years to come
when the sun
ignites
above that town

. . . Sated traffic from the gold plateau,
fattened on highveld pastures,
strolls in for a weekend wallow
gorging the yawning avenues

Screened eyes against a splintered heat,
beach thieves with arrogant gait
spill stilted shadows
brazen on the burning sand

When the sun sparks above the bluff,
much chat of shark nets and whalers
with their bleeding evening catch,
while they blindly hog their lagers

No thoughts for anything but appetite
propels dreaming heads toward the dawn,
but for some a hint of conscience waking
diverts ego trips to nightmare fright . . .

Remembering,
always in the distance,
on the skyline,
unending snakes
of silent smoke,
marking the chugging
of steel and wheels,
the hiss and plunge
of piston thrust,
the syphon roar
of furnace blast,
the clang and clank
of men on metal

Remembering,
that day
a distant rumble
like fleeting thunder
tugged the air;
all eyes rolled up
to scan for storm,
but relentless blue
swung pure above
in endless reassurance

Then sudden, through
the roar of surf,
a counterpoint
of marching feet:
a sea that came
not from the sea,
a tide which swelled
against the tide,
waves that surged
to top the waves;
pouring out of
plant and mill,
over wall and wire,
out of each
exploiters web,
out of effluence
and stink of fumes,
out of hunger's bite
and death's desire,
out of wasting years
and years of waste

With only dust to lose,
fragmented muscles gathered,
uniting with bone and fibre,
alive with nerve and fire:
the heavers, shifters
pullers and benders,
the hewers, diggers
builders and binders,
the servers, drivers
and general providers

Arms staggered the air,
fists drummed the sky,
a crimson flag
cracked the afternoon.

We will
remember Durban in 73,
we will
remember Durban
in years to come
when the sun ignites
above that town.

MOONANSUN, MANANGUN

Think of those at home
those in gaol
those alone
moonansun
manangun

Think of thoughts to hear
thoughts to fire
thoughts to fear
moonansun
manangun

Doing is an act to be
a fact of life
necessity
moonansun
manangun

Tears are stranded on the moon
blood is storming in the sun
think and act
thought and done
moonansun moonansun
manangun.

STANDING ARMED ON OUR OWN GROUND

Remember the agony years
(will they ever pass?)
tears and blood like rain
(but we are still bleeding!)
This deluge dampened our fathers,
diluted our mothers' milk,
rendered tepid the heat of young sons.

The land waxed fat on plunder,
investors reaped thick harvest:
a thieves rule keyed to chains.
Man-bone hewn for paving stone
the marrow served as mortar,
man-sweat grew concrete towers
and muscle nourished millionaires.

Now looking back becalmed
piercing with sharp black eyes,
standing armed on our own ground
firm on our feet of steel,
we assess both cause and toll
and cost the sacred path
from casualty to liberty.

A. N. C. Kumalo

OX HOOVES TROD HEAVILY

Ox hooves trod heavily
upon our tongues
flattened
our childhood days
our childhood gaze
ground our generation
into the white ants' nest
but could not resist
Africa's sun
filtering through the crust
nibbling at the mind
could not flatten
indefinite
the curvature of earth
the oval shape
the globe.

THE LONG DROP

Look down
from a headlong-height
into a long drop
and know how Babla[1] died.

The long drop
a helpless fall
they said he jumped.

'That one?
He left by the window',
they casually boast
grinning into pain.

[1] *Babla Saloojee*

A man does not fall
like stone
there is blinding light
at the centre of an explosion.

Transfixed
the murderers stand
above the abyss.

A POEM OF VENGEANCE

Mini,
Big strong smiling Mini
and Khayinga and Mkaba[1] who loved life
no less, have been robbed
of their most precious possession,
life.

Our comrades fell
in Verwoerd's Pretoria
bitten in the neck
by the hangman's knot.

Have you seen life slipping away?
I once saw my mother die
on the sharp sand at Sharpeville.

I hear Babla my brother cry
and his body hitting concrete
one hundred feet down
from the interrogator's window.

Have you seen the face
of a man being beaten up?
In prison
when you hear the noise
your heart-beats race.

[1] *Three trade union leaders, members of the ANC,
hanged November 1964*

But worst of all
is the sigh
   or shriek
     or cough
       or nothing
just escaping air
as life slips away.

How did Mini and my brothers die
in that secret hanging place?
You may ask – please let me tell you –
I know.

Singing? Yes – but how they sing!
Big firm Mini
not smiling on this day
a smile at the lips perhaps
but the eyes grim
always grim
when facing the enemy.

Heads high they walk
strong united together
singing Mini's own song[1]
'Naants' indod' emnyama Verwoerd'
– Watch out Verwoerd the black man will get you –
'Watch out Verwoerd'
the people have taken up this song
'Watch out Verwoerd'
the world sings with Mini.

And meeting Death
in their front-line trench
the three heroes shout
into the grey teeth of the enemy
'We shall be avenged'
and the people take up the shout
'Our heroes shall be avenged.'

It is vengeance we want
as the last precious gasps
escape into the Pretoria air.

[1] *Vuyusile Mini was the composer of
many freedom songs*

BEFORE INTERROGATION?

(An Epitaph to Ahmed Timol and Others)

Their triumph when landing him
was like hooking a fish.
Four days later they told his father
go pray in the mosque
your son is dead
he has fallen from a window
we have lain him out on a slab.

Saloojee plunged from this spot
in 1964, they grinned at Timol
showing him the seven storey drop
like you he would not talk.

Smirking and winking
enjoying the sport
they led him three flights up;
do you like the view
are you ready to talk?
you're a prize catch
do you prefer the honour
of a bigger splash?

Playing him out
at the end of a line
he refused to break
under the striking rod;
patience ran out
in a sjambok rage
they flung him to ground
with a head-wheeling crash
that covered the marks of the gaff.

They spoke of the leap
like an Olympic feat;
we never use force
it was a matter of course
some hang themselves
some slip on soap
this one chose to jump.

The police mouthpiece
addressed the press
the seventeenth account of sudden death:
'We threaten no one
We assault no one
We assume that no one
would want to escape
no one
no one
no one.'

And flicking his tongue
he wrote an epitaph for all the dead:
'We know Communists
when violence is planned
commit suicide
rather than mention
their comrades names.
They are taught to jump out
before interrogation.'

ASSURANCE FROM THE JUSTICE MINISTER

Justice Minister Vorster[1]
with a thread of smile
between ghostly lips
says he visits his prisons
regularly
– like a doctor at the patient's bed –
and has nothing to hide.
Journalists and MP's are welcome
to tour.
They may touch the pulse
squint at the mercury
talk no doubt to the *healthiest*
generally spend an hour where men spend their lives
and publish anything.
Libel actions, perjury charges and
charges for offences
under the Prisons' Act
need not worry them.

[1] *J. B. Vorster held this position until
he became Prime Minister*

All the Act says
is that you may not publish
untrue stories.
That way you end up
like the three Afrikaans warders
who spoke to the press:
one under house arrest
the other two in lock-up.

The Justice Minister is fond
of that type of assurance.

CITY OF LONDON PROFIT MAN

(a jingle for the overseas investors in Apartheid)

City gent
   money gent
      profit man
         louse
stuffing your guts
                  with goose and grouse
golf and gin
            and dividends received
On what else does your belly feed?
FAT BUG!

From this pin-striped gent
                        we understand
black labour blows its nose in hand;
And what of his civilizing spree?
grabbing grub off every tree!
SWOLLEN BUG!

When infant dies of broken tummy
ain't
   kiddies
      dying
         bloody
            funny?

Has City gent his fill?
No!
  The profit man is gorging still!
BLOATED BUG!

City gent
  money gent
    profit man
      louse
pewking
      in his summer-house
be-gloved be-jewelled
                  tie-fidgeting breed
BEWARE!
      We'll put
        an end
          to greed . . .
POP!

RED OUR COLOUR

Let's have poems
blood-red in colour
ringing like damn bells.

Poems
that tear at the oppressors face
and smash his grip.

Poems that awaken man:

Life not death
Hope not despair
Dawn not dusk
New not old
Struggle not submission.

Poet
let the people know
that dreams can become
reality.

Talk of freedom
and let the plutocrat
decorate his parlour walls
with the perfumed scrawls of dilettantes.

Talk of freedom
and touch people's eyes
with the knowledge of the power
of multitudes
that twists prison bars like grass
and flattens granite walls like putty.

Poet
find the people
help forge the key
before the decade
                    eats the decade
                            eats the decade.

Mazisi Kunene

THIS DAY

Like any other day I came home
After the long dreadful hours at the segregated desks
Where the tyrant had tacked us on like butterflies.
Hungry as usual I was, my lips cracking,
Swollen with the mouthings of a slave's education.
I trotted down droning the long-forgotten requiems of
    my people
And songs sung underneath the collapsing mines,
Where four hundred are buried already without as much
    as a tear from the patented clubs.

This is my home, you see straggling underneath the tall
    buildings;
My mother is dead, my sister told me.
I still recall how I ran maddened by the news,
My two-year old brother wailing to the setting sun.
He was not alone. We the children of Sharpeville,
Like frightened nestlings when the thief climbs the tree
Scattered in the dark looking for them.
The pointed grass was covered in blood.
I stayed awake as through the crack
The scarlet skies mocked my grief:
I cried until the agony of my parent's face
Sang the hymn, our hymn, the Song of Liberty.

AFTERMATH

The rains will be levelling the mounds we have dedicated
    to liberty
The torrential mixture will raise the chest with the waves,
There will be thick summers smelling decay,
We shall be like mushrooms after thunderbolt
    postmortems.

Our day is longer than this swelling smoke
We shall endure, regrow from the uncultivated fields
Because we are the weeds on the oppressors nights.

Such shall be the day of our rising
This bulk of love shall be redivided
Nor shall we allow the stench of beggars at our homes.
This love, this freedom, belongs to us and our beggars
So you shall conform to your portion
Until at the end of the table our little brother shall
        swing his lot.

But for now I have made brief distance
Between the earth and the moon
By calling at evenings on those dim dawns
Which will be coming so long as we advance, brother,
        advance.

THOUGHT ON JUNE 26

Was I wrong when I thought
All shall be avenged?
Was I wrong when I thought
The rope of iron holding the neck of young bulls
Shall be avenged?
Was I wrong
When I thought the orphans of sulphur
Shall rise from the ocean?
Was I depraved when I thought there need not be love,
There need not be forgiveness, there need not be progress,
There need not be goodness on the earth,
There need not be towns of skeletons,
Sending messages of elephants to the moon?
Was I wrong to laugh asphyxiated ecstasy
When the sea rose like quicklime
When the ashes on ashes were blown by the wind
When the infant sword was left alone on the hill top?
Was I wrong to erect monuments of blood?
Was I wrong to avenge the pillage of Caesar?
Was I wrong? Was I wrong?
Was I wrong to ignite the earth

And dance above the stars
Watching Europe burn with its civilization of fire,
Watching America disintegrate with its gods of steel,
Watching the persecutors of mankind turn into dust
Was I wrong? Was I wrong?

ABUNDANCE

I possess a thousand thundering voices
With which I call you from the place of the sinking sun.
I call you from the shaking of branches
Where they dance with the tail of the wind.
You are the endless abundance
Singing with the lips of all generations.
You are like a trunk lush with branches in the lake
Whom the feller of woods felled in vain,
But sprouts with new buds in summer.
When it is loaded with fruit he comes again
And eats to saturation desiring to end its season;
But again and again the branches shoot forth with new
        seasons.

VENGEANCE

How would it be if I came in the night
And planted the spear in your side
Avenging the dead:
Those you have not known,
Those whose scars are hidden,
Those about whom there is no memorial,
Those you only remembered in your celebration?
We did not forget them.
Day after day we kindled the fire,
Spreading the flame of our anger
Round your cities,
Round your children,
Who will remain the ash-monuments
Witnessing the explosions of our revenge.

THE POLITICAL PRISONER

I desired to talk
And talk with words as numerous as sands,
The other side of the wire,
The other side of the fortress of stone.

I found a widow travelling
Passing the prisoners with firewood.
It is this woman who forbade me to sleep
Who filled me with dreams.

The dream is always the same.
It turns on an anchor
Until it finds a place to rest:
It builds its cobwebs from the hours.

One day someone arrives and opens the gate.
The sun explodes its fire
Spreading its flames over the earth,
Touching the spring of mankind.

Behind us there are mountains
Where the widow is abandoned.
She remains there unable to give birth
Priding herself only in the shadows of yesterdays.

Hugh Lewin

THE WEDDING

Solly Nathee
　　stood alone
　　on the koppie[1] overlooking his home.

Solly Nathee
　　alone on the koppie
　　stood watching his home
　　where his daughter was getting married.

The guests
　　at the home below
　　were feasting the bride and the groom.

Near Solly Nathee
　　on the koppie
　　sat the Special Branch[2]
　　watching
　　to see that Solly Nathee
　　banned from social gatherings
　　behaved himself
　　at his daughter's wedding.

The guests
　　at the home below
　　feasted the bride and the groom
　　then walked
　　one by one
　　up the koppie
　　to shake the hand of Solly Nathee.

Solly Nathee
　　at his daughter's wedding
　　stood on the koppie overlooking his home
　　alone.

[1] *koppie = hill*
[2] *Special Branch = political police*

47

BEHIND A BARRED WINDOW

Behind
   a barred window
      behind a high wall
watching
   a blood red
      Transvaal sun
rise
   brilliant through
      a distant bluegum
you fly
   high
      very high.

ANOTHER DAY

(for Bram Fischer)[1]

It was like any other day
from un-lock
   breakfast / wash-up / scrub / clean
   garden / lunch
   lock-up
   wash-up / scrub / clean
   shower / 4 o'clock supper
   lock-up
till un-lock next morning
any day every day
14 hour lock-up
every night

In the morning
we picked our 11 mielies[2]
10 for us 1 for the boer
which passed half an hour
and another half-hour passed
tearing off the husks

---

[1] *A leader of the South African Communist Party serving a life sentence*
[2] *Mielies = maize*

excited about our own-grown mielies
which we sent to be cooked for supper.
In the afternoon
we trimmed the 21 tomato bushes
and were pleased to see
how they were springing up
green with fruitfulness.

It was like any other day
   garden / lunch
   lock-up
   wash-up / scrub / clean
   shower / 4 o'clock supper
but just before supper
he was called
unexpectedly
for a visit
which means I said
   either something good
   or something bad
So he missed supper with us
and we took his mielie to his cell
to eat after his visit
   either something good
   or something bad

It was like any other day
   supper / lock-up
   alone
   cell alone
   for 14 hours

While we ate
he was in the room
where you peer at your visitors
through a 4 inch strip of perspex
boxed in by wood panels
with sound-boards
to make the tapes clear.
You have boere on your side
they have boere on their side.
They call it the visitors room

His brother
peering through the perspex
into the wooden box
told him:
    Your son died this morning.
through the perspex
into the wooden box
keeping the State secure
    Your son died this morning.

His supper I suppose was cold
by the time he got back to his cell
  alone
  after lock-up
  for the next 14 hours
  like any other day.

TOUCH

When I get out
I'm going to ask someone
  to touch me
  very gently please
  and slowly,
  touch me
  I want
  to learn again
  how life feels.

I've not been touched
for seven years
  for seven years
  I've been untouched
  out of touch
  and I've learnt
  to know now
  the meaning of
  untouchable.

Untouched – not quite
I can count the things
that have touched me

One: fists
At the beginning
  fierce mad fists
  beating beating
  till I remember
  screaming
  Don't touch me
  please don't touch me.

Two: paws
The first four years of paws
  every day
  patting paws, searching
  – arms up, shoes off
  legs apart –
  prodding paws, systematic
  heavy, indifferent
  probing away
  all privacy.

I don't want fists and paws
I want
  to want to be touched
  again
  and to touch,
  I want to feel alive
  again
  I want to say
  when I get out
Here I am
please touch me.

Oswald R. Mtshali

BOY ON A SWING

Slowly he moves
to and fro, to and fro,
then faster and faster
he swishes up and down.

His blue shirt
billows in the breeze
like a tattered kite.

The world whirls by:
east becomes west,
north turns to south;
the four cardinal points
meet in his head.

  Mother!
Where did I come from?
When will I wear long trousers?
Why was my father jailed?

MEN IN CHAINS

The train stopped
at a country station,

Through sleep curtained eyes
I peered through the frosty window,
and saw six men;
men shorn
of all human honour
like sheep after shearing,
bleating at the blistering wind,
'Go away! Cold wind! Go away!
Can't you see we are naked?'

They hobbled into the train
on bare feet,
wrists handcuffed,
ankles manacled
with steel rings like cattle at the abbatoirs
shying away from the trapdoor.

One man with a head
shaven clean as a potato
whispered to the rising sun,
a red eye wiped by a tattered
handkerchief of clouds,
'Oh! Dear Sun!
Won't you warm my heart
with hope?'
The train went on its way to nowhere.

A ROADGANG'S CRY

Pneumatic drills
roar like guns in a battle field
as they tear the street.

Puffing machines swallow the red soil
and spit it out like a tuberculotic's sputum.

Business bent brokers hurry past;
Women shoppers shamble tiredly, shooing their children;
Stragglers stop to stare
as the ruddy-faced foreman watches men
lifting a sewerage pipe into a trench.

It starts
as a murmur
from one mouth to another
in a rhythm of ribaldry
that rises to a crescendo
'Abelungu ngo'dam – Whites are damned
Basibiza ngo Jim – they call us Jim.'

GOING TO WORK

I go to work
for five days a week
with a thousand black bodies
encased in eleven coaches
that hurtle through stations
into the red ribbon of dawn
crowning the city skyscrapers.

A commuter mumbles
like a dreamer muffled
by a brandy nightcap
'Brothers, who doesn't know me . . . . ?
I'm a cog in Mr Jobstein's wheel,
And Mr Jobstein is a big wheel
Rolling under Mr de Wiel's oxwaggon.'

HANDCUFFS

Handcuffs
have steel fangs
whose bite is more painful
than a whole battalion
of fleas.

Though the itch in my heart
grows deeper and deeper
I cannot scratch.

How can I?
my wrists
are manacled.
My mind
is caged.
My soul
is shackled.

I can only grimace at the ethereal cloud,
a banner billowing in the sky, emblazoned,
'Have hope, brother,
despair is for the defeated.'

54

Arthur Nortje

AT LANSDOWNE BRIDGE

After the whoosh of doors slid shut
at Lansdowne Bridge I swim in echoes.
Who fouled the wall O people?
FREE THE DETAINEES someone wrote there.

Black letters large as life stare you
hard by day in the black face;
above the kikuye grass to the sandflats
goes the boorish clang-clang of railways.

Darkness neutralizes the request
till dawn falls golden and sweet,
though a sudden truck by night
cornering, holds it in spidery light.

COSMOS IN LONDON

Leaning over the wall at Trafalgar Square
we watch the spray through sun-drenched eyes,
eyes that are gay as Yeats has it:
the day suggests a photograph.
Pigeons perch on our shoulders as we pose
against the backdrop of a placid embassy,
South Africa House, a monument of granite.
The seeds of peace are eaten from our brown palms.

My friend in drama, his beady black eyes
in the Tally Ho saloon at Kentish Town:
we are exchanging golden syllables
between ensembles. I break off to applaud
a bourgeois horn-man. A fellow in a yellow
shirt shows thumbs up: men are demonstrative.
While big-eyed girls with half-pints stand
our minds echo sonorities of elsewhere.

55

One time he did Macbeth
loping across like a beast in Bloemfontein
(Othello being banned along with Black Beauty),
The crowd cheered, they cheered also
the witches, ghosts: that moment you could feel
illiteracy drop off them like a scab.
O come back Africa! But tears may now
extinguish even the embers under the ash.

There was a man who broke stone
next to a man who whistled Bach.
The khaki thread of the music emerged
in little explosions from the wiry bodies.
Entranced by the counterpoint
the man in the helmet rubbed his jaw
with one blond hand, and with the other
pinned the blue sky up under his rifle,

Tobias should be in London. I could name
Brutus, Mandela, Lutuli – but that memory
disturbs the order of the song, and whose
tongue can stir in such a distant city?
The world informs her seasons, and she,
solid with a kind of grey security.
selects and shapes her own strong tendencies.
We are here, nameless, staring at ourselves.

It seems at times as if I am
this island's lover, and can sing her soul,
away from the stuporing wilderness where
I wanted the wind to terrify the leaves.
Peach aura of faces without recognition,
voices that blossom and die bring need for death.
The rat-toothed sea eats rock, and who escapes
a lover's quarrel will never rest his roots.

AUTOPSY

1

My teachers are dead men. I was too young
to grasp their anxieties, too nominal an exile
to mount such intensities of song;
knowing only the blond
colossus vomits its indigestible
black stepchildren like autotoxins.

Who can endure the succubus?
She who had taught them proudness of tongue
drank an aphrodisiac, then swallowed
a purgative to justify the wrong.
Her iron-fisted ogre of a son
straddled the drug-blurred townships,
breathing hygienic blasts of justice.

Rooted bacteria had their numbers
swiftly reduced in the harsh sunlight of arc-lamps,
the arid atmosphere where jackboots scrape
like crackling electric, and tape recorders
ingest forced words like white corpuscles,
until the sterile quarantine of dungeons
enveloped them with piteous oblivion.

In the towns I've acquired
arrive the broken guerrillas, gaunt and cautious,
exit visas in their rifled pockets
and no more making like Marx
for the British Museum in the nineteenth century,
damned: the dark princes, burnt and offered
to the four winds, to the salt-eyed seas. To their earth
unreturnable,
          The world receives
them, Canada, England now that the laager
masters recline in a gold inertia
behind the arsenal of Sten guns. I
remember many, but especially one
almost poetic, so undeterrable.

2

He comes from knife-slashed landscapes:
I see him pounding in his youth across red sandfields
raising puffs of dust at his heels,
outclassing the geography of dongas
mapped by the ravenous thundery summers.
He glided down escarpments like the wind, until
pursued by banshee sirens
he made their wails the kernel of his eloquence,
turning for a time to irrigate
the stretches of our virgin minds.

Thus – sensitive precise
he stood with folded arms in a classroom
surveying a sea of galvanized roofs,
transfixed as a chessman, only
with deep inside his lyric brooding,
the flame-soft bitterness of love that recrudesces;
O fatal loveliness of the land
seduced the laager masters to disown us.

36,000 feet above the Atlantic
I heard an account of how they had shot
a running man in the stomach. But what isn't told
is how a warder kicked the stitches open
on a little-known island prison which used to be
a guano rock in a sea of diamond blue.

Over the phone in a London suburb he sounds
grave and patient – the years have stilled him:
the voice in a dawn of ash, moon-steady,
is wary of sunshine which has always been
more diagnostic than remedial.

The early sharpness passed beyond to noon
that melted brightly into shards of dusk.
The luminous tongue in the black world
has infinite possibilities no longer.

ASSEVERATIONS

The fire will not ask me to make its bed,
nor is there more than one room in the womb:
cold stone stands above you or instead
your ashes have been scattered in the wind.

Drops of compassion in the oceans of
humanity are bitterly invisible:
the rice-field and the rose-garden must blend
before the hand that sowed can waft in harvest.

Words I plant in this cool adversity
germinate in April ardour, green
fused push through sleep mist that has haunted
the rich black soil of midnight in the brain,

I ghost-wrote tales in Africa, pseudonymous and,
hunched in shack or hovel in pursuit
of truths in rhythms, nocturnes, melodies:
grappled with the hardship of a rhyme.

The liberators are unnamable,
with winter in their hair perhaps, themselves
hexed, or fallen in the rape of grass,
whose recipes are now illegible.

Out of such haze, such loss, the luck of birth,
must be fashioned never questionably
strength of seed and courage of decision.
There is never work without resistance.

NATIVE'S LETTER

Habitable planets are unknown or too
far away from us to be
of consequence. To be of
value to his homeland must the wanderer

not weep by northern waters, but love
his own bitter clay
roaming through the hard cities, tough
himself as coffin nails.

Harping on the nettles of his melancholy,
keening on the blue strings of the blood,
he will delve into mythologies perhaps
call up spirits through the night.

Or carry memories apocryphal
of Tshaka, Hendrik Witbooi, Adam Kok,[1]
of the Xhosa nation's dream
as he moonlights in another country:

but he shall also have
cycles of history
outnumbering the guns of supremacy.

Now and wherever he arrives
extending feelers into foreign scenes
exploring times and lives,
equally may he stand and laugh,
explode with a paper bag of poems,
burst upon a million televisions
with a face as in a Karsh photograph,
slave voluntarily in some siberia
to earn the salt of victory.

Darksome, whoever dies
in the malaise of my dear land
remember me at swim,
the moving waters spilling through my eyes:

and let no amnesia
attack at fire hour:
for some of us must storm the castles
some define the happening.

[1] *Leaders of black resistance to white colonization*

QUESTIONS AND ANSWERS

1 *Questions and answers*
The underbelly of the shark shows when
song stops
and the reed that harped the wind
snaps.
Which Dutch Reformed Churchman has the sheer gall
not to compensate the looted Kaffir?
I asked at the golden portals
and no one answered me, not one
I asked at the broken gates.

2 *After war, after poverty*
We have become effigies, camera pabulum,
ineffectual scarecrows guarding the corn.
    And the dead point their fingers at some growing girl:
    she shall have tin cans slung from her shoulders,
    she shall have leaden balls on her toes.
We are caught
in colourful postures at shanty entrances
with corrugated faces trapped in Kodacolor.
The Information Bureau do not tell you who
is sweeping Parliament floors after the great
incomprehensible debates of the Potchefstroom Doctors:
the Bloemfontein farmers have more to say
about where I must live and work than
Adam Kok's descendants or Nelson Mandela the lawyer
who because of the golden words that sprang from his
    black mouth
languishes in a stone cage and may not even
try to swim the Hellespont to Capetown.

3 *I do not to salvation move*
I have broken free of those excellent unctions
administered in the name of my country's honour.
I have rejected the domains of gold
because I was living with the burning devil:
    (Apollo was martyred by the masters
    and the keepers of the keys of the kingdom

made us eat husks and baboon-flesh
while they drank the nectar)
Rimbaud's nightmares or the evil flowers
that sprout in the festering alleys of Johannesburg
proclaim the blackmass I will hold
        (and who shall stop me, Charles Engelhard?)
I will not to salvation move
being transplanted from here to there
endorsed out to some alien native land
        (Cape Town to Transkei on the night train:
        Matanzima ruled there a land
        of eroded paupers)
I will not slip across the border
patrolled by men with leashed Alsatians
snarling along the barbed wire fences
looking for a disturber of something or other:
I am no guerilla.
I will fall out of the sky as the Ministers gape from their
        front porch
and in broad daylight perpetrate atrocities
on the daughters of the boss:
ravish like Attila
and so acquire more scars myself
laughing as I infest the vulnerable liberals
with the lice inherited from their gold-mine fathers
        (Cecil John Rhodes must not expect an apology
        and I cannot but condole with Anton Rupert)
I have dug enough diamonds for them
in the blue pipes of Kimberley:
foreign crowns were studded with the stones of my sweat
        (where is that piece of glass picked up by a Native
        and christened the Cullinan Diamond?
        They say it was expertly cut for Queen Victoria,
        that imperious German lady)

4 *There is none innocent*
What are the 'thousands of innocents caught in the cross-
        fire'
doing just standing there
on this vast battlefield
        (British and American nationals I am afraid
        cannot be evacuated from city hotels

where the fighting is fiercest: no Viscount, no Boeing
   727,
no Red Cross mercy flight can land on one of those
   office blocks
47 storeys high, gilt edge investment).
Besides the scorpion that seldom stirs
has plenty of work to do:
   (where is thy sting?)
Because the lion lies lazily now in the Kruger National
   Park
or only stalks the zoo
the hyena laughs:
   (but for how long?)
Not for an eternity can such because I too
come pulsing here with prowess.
Taxed by these Herrenvolk pronunciamentoes
breathed by a fiery Sunday diaken
'We will fight till the blood is to the horse's nostrils'
I laugh myself to death that they should find
flesh no longer grass.
But forbiddingly we must issue a caveat to all the
   disinterested:
'This is not Biafra or Amman.
and the river cannot be crossed
once the tears are in spate.'

5 *Exile from the first*
Exile was implanted
in the first pangs of paradise. This land became
a refuge for adventurers.
And who remembers history
need not trouble my
head with tales. I underwent the fire
baptism, reared in rags, schooled
in the violence of the mud.

God's truth regardless of the death's rattle
(I come to execute what's pertinent)
or your stupendous array of guns
or the echelons of Stellenbosch cadets.
Effective immediately, stormtroopers
will be on recall from Rhodesian campaigns

and the Caprivi Strip will revert to peaceful marshland,
the base to keep watch on Zambia there
will be as much of a launching pad
as the rotting walls of Zimbabwe.
Those ramparts will break like so many reeds,
these towers tumble in a hail of stones.

For such were this Eldorado's
rife iniquities
that one would speculate
its hydra-headed births derive
from the malice of the sun
coupled with the boermeid's[1] stern maternity:
white trash
coursing through my blood
for all the unalienable seasons,
and I have an incurable
malaise that makes me walk
restlessly
through the sewers of these distant cities.

Who but to save me but myself?
I bred words in hosts, in vain, I'll have to
bleed: bleed for the broken mountains, lost
Umshlanga, Hangklip, Winterberg,
the starving rivers wait for me to plunge through
to the forefront,
the mud has hardened on my boots.
Ancestors will have their graves uprooted,
uncouth will be the interrogations and bloody the reprisals.

[1] *Boermeid = young Afrikaner woman*

Cosmo Pieterse

ANNEALED MICROPOLIS

Our karroo now has midwinter as its heart:

This sky of wintertime's cloudless –
Earth dry
Over its grey
Vastness
Hunger drives
Gaunt flocks like
Darkened
Clouds of storm to graze.
The waterpipes and taps
And the land's pulse are locked
In ice.

Summer brings lightning sudden thunder storms:
annulling and healing cold drought, in November.

SONG (We Sing)

We sing our sons who have died red
Crossing the sky where barbed wire passes
Bullets of white paper, nails of grey lead
And we sing the moon in its dying phases.

We sing the moon, nine blue moons of being
We sing the moons of barren blood
Blood of our daughters, waters fleeing
From bodiless eyes, that have stared and dried.

The seed of the land we sing, the flowers
Of manhood, of labour, of spring:
We sing the deaths that we welcome as ours
And the birth from the dust that is green we sing.

GUERILLA

I sometimes feel a cold love burning
Along the shuddering length of all my spine;
It's when I think of you with some kind of yearning,
Mother, stepmotherland, who drops your litter with
    a bitter spurning
And then I know, quite quietly and sure, just how
Before the land will take new seed, even before
    we forge a single plough,
We'll have to feel one sharp emotion deep, resolve
    one deed:
That we must march over the length of all your
    life, transgressing your whole body with harsh
                    boots upon our feet.

MIDSUMMER SLEEP AND ZIMBABWE BATTLEFIELD

Listening grey with seed-spill
It is high time a low spirit
Fell and crawled where the weeds fell
Lie low-crept like some slinking ferret
Spying out the land well
Sunk into the soil till
The earth with ears inherit
Can broadcast and all tell
Where the first who stir it
Still made fertile drill
By mark time their green cell
We shall mark it, disinter it
When morning is lustrousness on the pearl shell
Now pour it.

IN MAN LIES ALL HIS REVOLUTION

(for B. F.–who may have died near the Zimbabwe River)

February
Each young man dead
    in your youth
    every new year
    every
February briefly refracts our climates and seasons
    for your skull covers various
       dimensions different
          hemisphere comradely
            for comeliness
  is the flagrant bed
    of the mourning sheets ·
      the yellow
              seeds
fallow   in the ripe brain
  but by the feather-arrow
     forensically
       logistically
         done to death
           bullet
               showering you from your
                   splintered head
              brothering the flower
                we wear
                  brother
              we swear
                   LIFE
         Basil.

Mongane Wally Serote

CITY JOHANNESBURG

This way I salute you:
My hand pulses to my back trousers pocket
Or into my inner jacket pocket
For my pass,[1] my life,
Jo'burg City.
My hand like a starved snake rears my pockets
For my thin, ever lean wallet,
While my stomach groans a friendly smile to hunger,
Jo'burg City.
My stomach also devours coppers and papers
Don't you know?
Jo'burg City, I salute you;
When I run out, or roar in a bus to you,
I leave behind me, my love,
My comic houses and people, my dongas[2] and my
    ever whirling dust,
My death,
That's so related to me as a wink to the eye.
Jo'burg City
I travel on your black and white and roboted[3] roads,
Through your thick iron breath that you inhale,
At six in the morning and exhale from five noon.
Jo'burg City
That is the time when I come to you,
When your neon flowers flaunt from your electrical wind,
That is the time when I leave you,
When your neon flowers flaunt their way through the
    falling darkness

[1] *Pass = identification document which Africans are forced
to carry at all times. Failure to produce a pass on demand
means certain imprisonment*
[2] *Dongas = ditches*
[3] *Robots = traffic lights*

On your cement trees.
And as I go back, to my love,
My dongas, my dust, my people, my death,
Where death lurks in the dark like a blade in the flesh,
I can feel your roots, anchoring your might, my feebleness
In my flesh, in my mind, in my blood,
And everything about you says it,
That, that is all you need of me.
Jo'burg City, Johannesburg,
Listen when I tell you,
There is no fun, nothing, in it,
When you leave the women and men with such frozen
    expressions,
Expressions that have tears like furrows of soil erosion,
Jo'burg City, you are dry like death,
Jo'burg City, Johannesburg, Jo'burg City.

WHAT'S IN THIS BLACK 'SHIT'

It is not the steaming little rot
In the toilet bucket,
It is the upheaval of the bowels
Bleeding and coming out through the mouth
And swallowed back,
Rolling in the mouth,
Feeling its taste and wondering what's next like it.

Now I'm talking about this;
'Shit' you hear an old woman say,
Right there, squeezed in her little match-box[1]
With her fatness and gigantic life experience,
Which makes her a child,
'Cause the next day she's right there,
Right there serving tea to the woman
Who's lying in bed at 10 a.m. sick with wealth,
Which she's prepared to give her life for
'Rather than you marry my son or daughter.'

[1] *Match-box = tiny outhouse in the yard
of a white residence where black servants
live.*

This 'Shit' can take the form of action;
My younger sister under the full weight of my father,
And her face colliding with his steel hand,
"Cause she spilled sugar that I work so hard for'
He says, not feeling satisfied with the damage his hands
Do to my yelling little sister.

I'm learning to pronounce this 'Shit' well,
Since the other day,
At the pass office,
When I went to get employment,
The officer there endorsed me to Middleburg,
So I said, hard and with all my might, 'Shit!'
I felt a little better;
But what's good, is, I said it in his face,
A thing my father wouldn't dare do.
That's what's in this black 'Shit'.

THE GROWING

No!
This is not dying when the trees
Leave their twigs
To grow blindly long into windows like fingers into eyes.
And leave us unable
To wink or to blink or to actually close the eye,
The mind –
Twigs thrusting into windows and leaves falling on the
      sills,
Are like thoughts uncontrolled and stuffing the heart.
Yes,
This is teaching about the growing of things:
If you crowd me I'll retreat from you,
If you still crowd me I'll think a bit,
Not about crowding you but about your right to crowd
      me;
If you still crowd me, I will not, but I will be thinking
About crowding you.
If my thoughts and hands reach out
To prune the twigs and sweep the leaves,

70

There was a growth of thought here,
Then words, then action.
So if I say prune instead of cut,
I'm teaching about the growing of things.

HELL, WELL, HEAVEN

I do not know where I have been,
But Brother,
I know I'm coming.
I do not know where I have been,
But Brother,
I know I heard the call.
Hell! where I was I cried silently
Yet I sat there until now.
I do not know where I have been,
But Brother,
I know I'm coming:
I come like a tide of water now,
But Oh! there's sand beneath me!
I do not know where I have been
To feel so weak, Heavens! so weary.
But Brother,
Was that Mankunku's[1] horn?
Hell! my soul aches like a body that has been beaten,
Yet I endured till now.
I do not know where I have been,
But Brother,
I know I'm coming.
I do not know where I have been,
But Brother I come like a storm over the veld,
And Oh! there are stone walls before me!
I do not know where I have been
To have fear so strong like the whirlwind (will it be that
    brief?)
But Brother,
I know I'm coming.
I do not know where I have been,
But Brother,
Was that Dumile's[2] figure?
Hell, my mind throbs like a heart beat, there's no peace;

[1] *a musician*
[2] *a sculptor*

And my body of wounds – when will they be scars? –
Yet I can still walk and work and still smile.
I do not know where I have been
But Brother,
I know I'm coming.
I do not know where I have been,
But Brother,
I have a voice like the lightning-thunder over the
    mountains.
But Oh! there are copper lightning conductors for me!
I do not know where I have been
To have despair so deep and deep and deep
But Brother,
I know I'm coming.
I do not know where I have been
But Brother.
Was that Thoko's[1] voice?
Hell, well, Heavens!

[1] *a singer*

MY BROTHERS IN THE STREETS

Oh you black boys,
You thin shadows who emerge like a chill in the night,
You whose heart-tearing footsteps sound in the night,
My brothers in the streets,
Who holiday in jails,
Who rest in hospitals,
Who smile at insults,
Who fear the whites,
Oh you black boys,
You horde-waters that sweep over black pastures,
You bloody bodies that dodge bullets,
My brothers in the streets,
Who booze and listen to records,
Who've tasted rape of mothers and sisters,
Who take alms from white hands,
Who grab bread from black mouths,
Oh you black boys,
Who spill blood as easy as saying 'Voetsek'[1]

[1] *Voetsek = bugger off*

Listen!
Come my black brothers in the streets,
Listen,
It's black women who are crying.

MOTIVATED TO DEATH

We knew each other well.
He was my brother;
Now he's dead.
The RSA[1] condemned him
Not Alex[2] – where he died, where his killers exist.
No!
His crime? (Thanks, he's beyond this now).
He had no pass. Didn't work, had nowhere to stay.
His meals? He shared beer with friends.
His death-bed, a muddy donga,
His blankets, the dewy green grass,
Yes, now it's over, he's silent and unconcerned.
Quiet!
Death the knife cut the flesh.
Time the heat dried his blood.
It was clear to him, alone in the donga,
He was dying;
That gash on his right hip bled
His black miseries to the core of silence.
Me I want to believe
That they that kill by knife
Shal! so die.

Even in Alex?

[1] *RSA = Republic of South Africa*
[2] *Alex = Alexandra, a black ghetto*
outside Johannesburg

I WILL WAIT

I have tasted, ever so often,
Hunger like sand on my tongue
And tears like flames have licked my eye-lids
Blurring that which I want to see,
I want to know.
But Oh! often, now and then, everywhere where I have
　　been,
Joy, as real as paths,
Has spread within me like pleasant scenery,
Has run beneath my flesh like rivers glitteringly silver;
And now I know:
Having been so flooded and so dry,
I wait.

Scarlet Whitman

HOMECOOKED SUN-DRIED

Beasts are preying in our land
not stately elephant
or elegant leopard.
part of nature's pattern,
but homecooked, sun-dried
closecropped
skinscrubbed
chinchucking
churchgoing
monomanic
misanthropes.

PURE WHITE, ONLY WHITE

Immigrant workers at Capetown's door
are questioned as follows
before flooding ashore:

Are you pure white, only white
or sadly partly white?
Real brown, only brown
or rough and reddy-brown?
Pitch black, dark black
or pale and fading black?
only untinted are ever invited
only unstained are ever retained
This includes your mind in abstraction
What you think
What you feel
If inclined to distraction.

Turned back at gang plank all sundry faces
all weathered complexions, all unshaven traces
Those uncertain of brilliance of sheen
must produce in a flash a convincing picture
of parents plan and grandfather's sister.

A surprise for the filtered
when apprised of the scene
is that experts appraising
are grey faced or green.

THIS IS JOHNNY

Of an umbre hue
under dense hedge of hair,
his eyes intimate,
warmth showing,
teeth spark intermittently
through close black strands
of clotted beard.
A ragged rift of scar,
dark purple stained,
scowls an unlined forehead
ramming a swollen fold
low over right eye socket.

This is Johnny
our resting representative
hot from the Sahara;
recently lacerated
on a rough sand road:
big tree reared up
and renault somersaulted,
he perhaps thrown clear
but driver dead outright.
An Algerian miracle recorded.
Their broken bodies
gathered local peasants
wailing one freedom fighter,
where dying Frenchmen
didn't stir a tear.

After a fortnight of fog,
bed besieged by shaky apparitions,
he flew to London to recouperate.
En route to airport
men from FLN
offered a glance
at cars crumpled carcass
but wiseness steered him clear.

He says 'Its funny
what unconscious does
while deep in coma,
my memory is
what makes me after all:
French and English quite forgotten
used Zulu in my every day
clicking[1] Algerians into a muzzle.
A minister chided me
for not teaching him that tongue.'

Now repairing again,
pulled back from utter blackness,
we, in fun, said to live it up,
once plucked from edge
throw caution to the wind!
He laughed out loud,
remembering quietly,
and everyone recalled then
with much animation,
many more such
and other collisions
from shifting sands, south,
three thousand miles.

[1] *The click sound is common in Zulu speech*

ALL WENT MAGNIFICENT IN '21

(On 50th Anniversary of the South African Communist Party)

We address our people's cause
to ourselves, as our beginning
in a micro-probe of five decades.
Moments wrested from movements
compressed in the trap of time,
ensnaring bold emotions
grasping relayed actions;
life's hunter stalking 50 years.

The fight did not begin in '21
it only incorporated.
Whatever bleeding preceded
and there was much blood,
whatever celebrations receded
and there was much to sing about,
all went magnificent in '21.

Now full tilt at fifty,
decades ahead flush red from our eyes,
the clapping of our guns
curtain-calls the fisted years.

POWDERED TYPHOONS UNWIND SLOWLY

Leaving a day stunned with sun,
a still evening sky of battle zone
cools the steel of our eager guns.
The air clear, no clutter of vision;
no cold nip deters the simmered spirit,
only wild odoured earth
hard, dry and dust bedecked,
a mindful scent of timeless continent.
Here elephants roll and spray
dark hides pumiced by sprinkled rock
and roaming herds kick up ochre clouds.
Without a wind or sudden rain
powdered typhoons unwind slowly.

78

Pushing through the scratch of bush
a dark green file of dipping backs,
pulled low by shoulder strap abrasion
and weight of arms in harnessed cradle.
The chant of life from hidden branches
signals a pause then progress of the line.

No man but shadows from the past
traced steps through this ancient track;
centuries of suffering equip for pain
centuries of dying dry the verging tear
centuries of fighting steel this final test.
Yet each heart feels its passion thumping
each mind seeks out its reason fresh
each man sees with eyes of thunder
each man must be a lightning strike.

First a bite at white battalions
then on to breach the dam wall door.

AND SWEET SMELL OF DUST DEFEATED

Clouds are contrast to the sky,
not incongruous but in colour,
and more divided than united blue.
They move about almost unnoticed,
only poets dream their metaphor
scanning shapes to jog our empathy,
and weathermen judge their shuffling flight
to make equations of unlikely rain.

Storm clouds defy all prediction;
near bursting they mount up united,
fast on eye swept horizons,
recruiting humble reefs of steam
and rush in perceptible fury
masking out the sun
and in one menacing moment
envelop the day.

Depending on prevailing wind
the storm can merge into the night,
reforming darkness out of light,
or flash past to flood again
leaving a blinking sun, abluted sky
and sweet smell of dust defeated.

Biographical Notes

DENNIS BRUTUS
Brutus was born in 1924 in Salisbury, Rhodesia. He left South Africa for London in 1966 after serving eighteen months hard labour and a year under house arrest. His poems have appeared in numerous periodicals and anthologies. His first book, *Sirens, Knuckles, Boots*, was published by Mbari in 1964; since then he has published *Letters to Martha* (Heinemann, 1968) and *A Simple Lust* (Heinemann, 1973). Brutus, President of the South African Non-Racial Olympic Committee, is now Professor of English at North-Western University, Chicago.

BARRY FEINBERG
Feinberg was born in 1938 in Germiston, Transvaal, and has been living in London since 1961. His poems have appeared in various periodicals and anthologies including *Sechaba*, *Anti-Apartheid News*, *Sanity*, *Lotus*, *Guerilla Warfare* and *Apartheid*. Feinberg is also a painter and illustrator and has had several exhibitions in London.

A. N. C. KUMALO
Kumalo (a pseudonym) currently lives in London. His poems have appeared in *Sechaba*, *The African Communist*, *Transition*, *Pan Africa* and *Anti-Apartheid News*. He has also published short stories and articles in various African periodicals.

MAZISI KUNENE
Kunene was born in 1932 in Durban. Natal. and has lived in London since 1959. His poems have appeared in numerous periodicals and have been anthologized in several collections of African poetry. He wrote an introduction to the English edition of Ame Cesaire's *Return to the Native Land*. His first book, *Zulu Poems*, was published by Andre Deutsch in 1971. Kunene is also well known as an authority on African art and literature through his essays and lectures on radio and television.

81

HUGH LEWIN

Lewin was born in 1939 in the Eastern Transvaal. He came to London after serving a seven-year prison sentence for sabotage activities. His poems have appeared in *Sechaba* and *Lotus*. He worked as a journalist for *Post* and *Drum* in Johannesburg, and in London he is information officer of the International Defence and Aid Fund. *Bandiet*, an account of his gaol experiences, is published by Barrie and Jenkins.

OSWALD R. MTSHALI

Mtshali was born in 1940 in Vryheid, Natal and now lives in Soweto, Johannesburg. His poems have appeared in various periodicals and anthologies, including *Classic*, *New Coin Poetry*, *Purple Renoster*, *Ophir*, *New Nation* and PEN's *New South African Writing*. His first book, *Sounds of a Cowhide Drum*, was published by Renoster Books, Johannesburg, and Oxford University Press, London, in 1971. Mtshali was invited to read his poetry at the International Festival of Poetry in London in 1973.

ARTHUR NORTJE

Nortje was born in 1942 in Oudtshoorn, Cape Province. He came to England in 1966, and died in tragic circumstances in 1970 while studying for his doctorate at Oxford University. His poems have appeared in *Sechaba*, *Lotus*, *Apartheid* and *Seven South African Poets*. Nortje's collected poems were published posthumously as *Dead Roots* by Heinemann in 1973.

COSMO PIETERSE

Pieterse was born in 1930 in South West Africa, and has been based in London since 1965. While in South Africa he was banned in 1962 under the Riotous Assemblies Act. His poems have appeared in various periodicals and anthologies including *Lotus* and *Apartheid*. He has compiled and edited several volumes of African literature, including *Five African Plays* and *Seven South African Poets*, both published by Heinemann. Pieterse is also well known as an actor both on stage and radio.

MONGANE WALLY SEROTE

Serote was born in 1944 in Sophiatown, Johannesburg, and now lives in Alexandra. Johannesburg. He was imprisoned under the Terrorism Act in June 1969 and released nine months later without having been charged. His poems have appeared in various periodicals including *Classic, Purple Renoster, New Coin Poetry* and *Ophir*. His first book of poems, *Yakhal 'inkomo* (the cry of cattle at the slaughterhouse), was published by Renoster Books in Johannesburg in 1972.

SCARLET WHITMAN

Whitman (a pseudonym) currently lives in London. His poems have appeared in *The African Communist*.